THE WRITINGS OF ST. PATRICK

REV. CHARLES H.H. WRIGHT

Professor at the University of London

Professor at the University of Wales

Vicar of Saint John's, Liverpool

Dalcassian
Publishing
Company

PHILADELPHIA, PA

Library of Congress Cataloging-in-Publication Data

Copyright © 2020 Dalcassian Publishing Co.
All rights reserved.

THE CONFESSION OF ST. PATRICK.

THE BEGINNING OF THE BOOKS OF THE BISHOP ST. PATRICK.

I, Patrick, a sinner, the rudest and least of all the faithful, and most contemptible to very many, had for my father Calpornius, a deacon, the son of Potitus, a priest, who lived in Bannaven Taberniae, for he had a small country-house close by, where I was taken captive when I was nearly sixteen years of age. I knew not the true God, and I was brought captive to Ireland with many thousand men, as we deserved; for we had forsaken God, and had not kept His commandments, and were disobedient to our priests, who admonished us for our salvation. And the Lord brought down upon us the anger of His Spirit, and scattered us among many nations, even to the ends of the earth, where now my littleness may be seen amongst strangers. And there the Lord showed me my unbelief, that at length I might remember my iniquities, and strengthen my whole heart towards the Lord my God, who looked down upon my humiliation, and had pity upon my youth and ignorance, and kept me before I knew him, and before I had wisdom or could distinguish between good and evil, and strengthened and comforted me as a father would his son.

Therefore I cannot and ought not to be silent concerning the great benefits and graces which the Lord has bestowed upon me in the land of my captivity, since the only return we can make for such benefits is, after God has reproved us, to extol and confess His wonders before every nation under heaven.

For there is no other God, nor ever was, nor shall be hereafter, except the Lord, the unbegotten Father, without beginning, by whom all things have their being, who upholds all things, as we have said; and His Son, Jesus Christ, whom, together with the Father, we testify to have always existed before the origin of the world, spiritually with the Father, ineffably begotten before every beginning; and by Him were the visible things made—was made man, death being overthrown, in the heavens. And he hath given Him all power over every name of things in heaven and earth and hell, that every tongue should confess to Him that Jesus Christ is Lord, and whose coming we expect ere long to judge the living and dead; who will render to every one according to his works; who hath poured forth abundantly on us both the gift of His Spirit and the pledge of immortality; who makes the faithful and obedient to become the sons of God and coheirs with Christ; whom we confess and adore one God in the Trinity of the holy Name. For He Himself has said by the prophet: "Call upon me in the day of thy trouble: I will deliver thee, and thou shalt magnify me." And again he says: "It is honorable to reveal and confess the works of God."

Although I am imperfect in many things, I wish my brothers and acquaintances to know my dispositions, that they may be able to understand the desire of my soul. I am not ignorant of the testimony of my Lord, who declares in the psalm: "Thou wilt destroy all that speak a lie." And again: "The mouth that belieth, killeth the soul." And the same Lord: "Every idle word that men shall speak, they shall render an account for it in the Day of Judgment." Therefore, I ought, with great fear and trembling, to dread this sentence in that day when no one shall be able to withdraw or hide himself, but all must give an account, even of the least sins, before the judgment-seat of the Lord Christ.

Therefore, although I thought of writing long ago, I feared the censure of men, because I had not learned as the others who studied the sacred writings in the best way, and have never changed their language since their childhood, but continually learned it more perfectly, while I have to translate my words and speech into a foreign tongue; and it can be easily proved from the style of my writings how I am instructed in speech and learning, for the Wise Man says: "By the tongue wisdom is discerned, and understanding and knowledge and learning by the word of the wise." But what avails an excuse, however true, especially when accompanied with presumption? For I, in my old age, strive after that which I was hindered from learning in my youth. But who will believe me? And if I say what I have said before, that as a mere youth, nay, almost a boy in words, I was taken captive, before I knew what I ought to seek and to avoid. Therefore I blush today and greatly dread to expose my ignorance, because I am not able to express myself briefly, with clear and well-arranged words, as the spirit desires and the mind and intellect point out. But if it had been given to me as to others, I would not have been silent for the recompense; and although it may seem to some who think thus that I put myself forward with my ignorance and too slow tongue, nevertheless it is written, "The tongues of stammerers shall speak readily and plain"; how much more ought we to undertake this who are the epistle of Christ for salvation unto the ends of the earth, written in pure heart, if not with eloquence, yet with power and endurance, "not written with ink, but with the Spirit of the living God"; and again the Spirit testifies, "Husbandry, it was ordained by the Most High."

Therefore I undertook this work at first, though a rustic and a fugitive, and not knowing how to provide for the future; but this I know for certain: that before I was humbled, I was like a stone lying in deep mire, until He who is powerful came, and in his mercy raised me up, and indeed again succored and placed me in His part; and therefore I ought to cry out loudly, and thank the Lord in some degree for all his benefits, here and after, which the mind of man cannot estimate. Therefore be amazed, both great and small who fear God; rhetoricians and ye of the Lord, hear and enquire who aroused me, a fool, from the midst of those who seem to be wise, and skilled in the law, and powerful in speech and in all things, and hath inspired me (if indeed I be such) beyond others, though I am despised by this world, so that, with fear and reverence and without murmuring, I should faithfully serve this nation, to whom the charity of Christ hath transferred me, and given me for my life, if I shall survive; and that at last with humility and truth I should serve them.

In the measure, therefore, of the faith of the Trinity it behoves me to distinguish without shrinking from danger, and to make known the gift of God and everlasting consolation, and, without fear, confidently to spread abroad the name of God everywhere, so that after my death I may leave it to my Gallican brethren and to my sons, many thousands of whom I have baptized in the Lord. And I was neither worthy nor deserving that the Lord should so favor me, his servant, after such afflictions and great difficulties, after captivity, after many years, as to grant me such grace for this nation—a thing which, still in my youth, I had neither hoped for nor thought of.

But after I had come to Ireland, I was daily tending sheep, and I prayed frequently during the day, and the love of God, and His faith and fear, increased in me more and more, and the spirit was stirred; so that in a single day I have said as many as a hundred prayers, and in the night nearly the same; so that I remained in the woods, and on the mountain, even before the dawn, I was roused to prayer, in snow, and ice, and rain, and I felt no injury from it, nor was there any slothfulness in me, as I see now, because the spirit was then fervent in me. And there one night I heard a voice, while I slept, saying to me: "Thou dost fast well; fasting thou shalt soon go to thy country." And again, after a very short time, I heard a response, saying to me: "Behold, thy ship is ready." And the place was not near, but perhaps about two hundred miles distant, and I had never been there, nor did I know anyone who lived there.

Soon after this, I fled, and left the man with whom I had been six years, and I came in the strength of the Lord, who directed my way for good; and I feared nothing until I arrived at that ship. And the day on which I came the ship had moved out of her place; and I asked to go and sail with them, but the master was displeased, and replied angrily: "Do not seek to go with us." And when I heard this, I went from them to go thither where I had lodged; and I began to pray as I went; but before I had ended my prayer, I heard one of them calling out loudly after me, "Come quickly, for these men are calling you"; and I returned to them immediately, and they began saying to me; "Come, we receive thee in good faith; make such friendship with us as you wish." And then that day I disdained to supplicate them, on account of the fear of God; but I hoped of them that they would come into the faith of Jesus Christ, for they were Gentiles; and this I obtained from them; and after three days, we reached land, and for twenty-eight days we journeyed through a desert, and their provisions failed, and they suffered greatly from hunger; and one day the master began to say to me: "What sayest thou, O Christian? Your God is great and all-powerful; why canst thou not, then, pray for us, since we are perishing with hunger, and may never see the face of man again?" And I said to them plainly: "Turn sincerely to the Lord my God, to whom nothing is impossible, that He may send us food on your way until ye are satisfied, for it abounds everywhere for Him." And with God's help it was so done; for, lo! a flock of swine appeared in the way before our eyes, and they killed many of them, and remained there two nights, much refreshed and filled with their flesh; for many of them had been left exhausted by the wayside. After this, they gave the greatest thanks to God, and I was honored in their eyes.

They also found wild honey, and offered me some of it, and one of them said: "This is offered in sacrifice, thanks be to God"; after this, I tasted no more. But the same night, while I was sleeping, I was strongly tempted by Satan (of which I shall be mindful as long as I shall be in this body), and there fell, as it were, a great stone upon me, and there was no strength in my limbs. And then it came into my mind, I know not bow, to call upon Elias, and at the same moment I saw the sun rising in the heavens; and while I cried out Elias with all my might, behold! the splendor of the sun was shed upon me, and immediately shook from me all heaviness. And I believe that Christ my Lord cried out for me; and I hope that it will be so in the day of my adversity, as the Lord testifies in the Gospel: "It is not you that speak," etc.

Sometime after, I was taken captive; and on the first night I remained with them I heard a divine response, saying: "You shall be two months with them"; and so it was. On the sixtieth night the Lord delivered me out of their hands, and on the road, He provided for us food, and fire, and dry weather daily, until on the fourteenth day we all came. As I have above mentioned, we journeyed twenty-eight days through a desert, and on the night of our arrival we had no provisions left.

And again, after a few years, I was with my relations in Britain, who received me as a son, and earnestly besought me that then, at least, after I had gone through so many tribulations, I would get nowhere out of them. And there I saw, in the midst of the night, a man who appeared to come from Ireland, whose name was Victorious, and he had innumerable letters with him, one of which he gave to me; and I read the commencement of the epistle containing "The Voice of the Irish"; and as I read aloud the beginning of the letter, I thought I heard in my mind the voice of those who were near the wood of Focluti, which is near the western sea; and they cried out: "We entreat thee, holy youth, to come and walk still amongst us." And my heart was greatly touched, so that I could not read any more, and so I awoke. Thanks be to God that, after very many years, the Lord hath granted them their desire!

And on another night, whether in me or near me God knows, I heard eloquent words which I could not understand until the end of the speech, when it was said: "He who gave His life for thee is He who speaks in thee"; and so I awoke full of joy. And again, I saw one praying within me, and I was, as it were, within my body, and I heard, that is, above the inner man, and there he prayed earnestly with groans. And I was amazed at this, and marveled, and considered who this could be who prayed in me. But at the end of the prayer, it came to pass that it was a bishop, and I awoke and remembered that the apostle said: "Likewise the Spirit also helpeth our infirmity, for we know not what we should pray for as we ought, but the Spirit Himself asketh for us with unspeakable groanings." And again: "The Lord is our advocate, who also maketh intercession for us." [And when I was tried by some of my elders, who came and spoke of my sins as an objection to my laborious episcopate, I was on that day sometimes strongly driven to fall away here and forever. But the Lord spared a proselyte and a stranger for His name's sake, and mercifully assisted me greatly in that affliction, because I was not entirely deserving of reproach. I pray God that they may not be found guilty of giving an occasion of sin; they found me after thirty years, and brought against me words that I had confessed before I was a deacon; from anxiety, with sorrow of mind, I told my dearest friend what I had done in my youth, in one day, nay, rather in one hour, because I was not then able to overcome. I know not, God knows, if I was then fifteen years of age, and from my childhood I did not believe in the living God, but remained in death and unbelief until I was severely chastised, and, in truth, I have been humbled by hunger and nakedness; and even now I did not come to Ireland of my own will until I was nearly worn out. But this proved a blessing to me, for I was thus corrected by the Lord, and he made me fit to be to-day that which was once far from my thoughts, so that I should care for the salvation of others, for at that time I had no thought even for myself.

And in the night of the day in which I was reproved for the things above mentioned, I saw in the night.] I saw in a vision of the night a writing without honor before me. And then I heard an answer saying to me, "We have heard with displeasure the face of the elect without a name." He did not say, "Thou hast badly seen," but "We have badly seen," as if he had there joined himself to me, as he said: "He that touches you is as he who toucheth the apple of my eye." Therefore, I give thanks to Him who comforted me in all things that He did not hinder me from the journey which I had proposed, and also as regards my work which I had learned of Christ. But from this thing I felt no little strength, and my faith was approved before God and man.

Therefore, I dare to say that my conscience does not reproach me now or for the future. I have the testimony of God now that I have not lied in the words, I have told you. [But I feel the more grieved that my dearest friend, to whom I would have trusted even my life, should have occasioned this. And I learned from certain brethren that, before this defense, when I was not present, nor even in Britain, and with which I had nothing to do, that he defended me in my absence. He had even said to me with his own lips: "Thou art going to be given the rank of bishop," though I was not worthy of it. How, then, did it happen to him that afterwards, before all people, good and bad, he should detract me publicly, when he had before this freely and gladly praised me? And the Lord, who is greater than all? I have said enough. Still, I ought not to hide the gift of God which he gave me in the land of my captivity, for I sought him earnestly then, and found him there, and He preserved me from all iniquity, I believe, through the indwelling of His Spirit, which worketh within me unto this day more and more. But God knows, if it were man who spoke this to me, I would perhaps be silent for the love of Christ.

Therefore I give unceasing thanks to my God, who preserved me faithful in the day of my temptation, so that I can to-day offer him sacrifice confidently—the living sacrifice of my soul to Christ my Lord, who preserved me from all my troubles, so that I may say to Him: "Who am I, O Lord! or what is my calling, that divine grace should have so wrought with me, so that to-day I can so rejoice amongst the nations, and magnify Thy name, wherever I am, not only in prosperity, but also in adversity?" and I ought to receive equally whatever happens to me, whether good or evil, giving God thanks in all things, who hath shown me that I should, undoubtingly, without ceasing, believe in Him who hath heard me though I am ignorant, and that I should undertake, in those days, so holy and wonderful a work, and imitate those of whom our Lord predicted of old that they should preach His Gospel to all nations for a testimony before the end of the world; which has been accomplished, as we have seen. Behold, we are witnesses that the Gospel has been preached to the limits of human habitation.]

But it is too long to detail my labors particularly, or even partially. I will briefly say how the good God often delivered me from slavery and from twelve dangers by which my soul was threatened, besides many snares, and what in words I cannot express, and with which I will not trouble my readers. But God knows all things, even before they come to pass [as he does me, a poor creature. Therefore, the divine voice very often admonished me to consider whence came this wisdom, which was not in me, who neither knew God nor the number of my days. Whence did I obtain afterwards the great and salutary gift to know or love God, and to leave my country and my relations, although many gifts were offered to me with sorrow and tears. And I offended many of my seniors then against my will. But, guided by God, I yielded in no way to them—not to me, but to God be the glory, who conquered in me, and resisted them all; so that I came to the Irish people to preach the Gospel, and bear with the injuries of the unbelieving, and listen to the reproach of being a stranger, and endure many persecutions, even to chains, and to give up my freedom for the benefit of others. And if I be worthy, I am ready to give up my life unhesitatingly and most cheerfully for His name, and thus, if the Lord permit, I desire to spend it even until my death.]

For I am truly a debtor to God, who has given me so much grace that many people should be born again to God through me, and that for them everywhere should be ordained priests for this people, newly come to the faith, which the Lord took from the ends of the earth, as He promised formerly by His prophets: "Our fathers falsely prepared idols, and there is no profit in them, to thee the Gentiles come and will say." And again: "I have set thee to be the light of the Gentiles, that thou mayest be for salvation unto the utmost parts of the earth." And thus I wait the promise of Him who never fails, as He promises in the Gospel: "They shall come from the east and the west [from the north and from the south], and shall sit down with Abraham and Isaac and Jacob." So we believe that the faithful shall come from all parts of the world.

Therefore we ought to fish well and diligently; as the Lord taught and said: "Come ye after me, and I will make you fishers of men." And again: "Behold, saith the Lord, I send many fishers and many hunters," etc. Therefore we should, by all means, set our nets in such a manner that a great multitude and a crowd may be caught therein for God, and that everywhere there may be priests who shall baptize and exhort a people who so need it and desire it; as the Lord teaches and admonishes in the Gospel, saying: "Going, therefore, teach ye all nations, baptizing them in the name of the Father and of the Son and of the Holy Ghost, even to the consummation of the world." And again: "Go ye into the whole world and preach the Gospel to every creature; he that believeth and is baptized shall be saved, but he that believeth not shall be condemned." The rest are examples. [And again: "This Gospel of the kingdom shall be preached in the whole world for a testimony to all nations, and then shall the consummation come." And again, the Lord, speaking by the prophet, says: "And it shall come to pass in the last days, saith the Lord, that I will pour out my spirit upon all flesh, and your sons and your daughters shall prophesy, your old men shall dream dreams, and your young men shall see visions. Moreover, upon my servants and handmaids in those days I will pour forth my spirit, and they shall prophesy." And Osee saith: "And I will say to that which was not my people: Thou art my people: and to her who hath not found mercy; and they shall say; Thou art my God. And in the place where I said to them, You are not my people, it shall be said to them, Ye are the sons of the living God."]

Wherefore behold how in Ireland they who never had the knowledge *of God, and hitherto only worshipped unclean idols, have lately become* the people of the Lord, and are called the sons of God. The sons of the Scoti and the daughters of princes are seen to be monks and virgins of Christ. [And there was one blessed Irish maiden, of adult age, noble and very beautiful, whom I baptized, and after a few days she came to us for a reason, and gave us to understand that she had received a command from God, and was informed that she was to become a virgin of Christ, and to draw near to God. Thanks be to God, six days after this she most excellently and eagerly entered on this state of life, which all the virgins of God now adopt, even against the will of their parents, even enduring reproaches and persecution from them, and notwithstanding they increase in number; and as for those who are born again in this way, we know not their number, except the widows and those who observe continency. But those who are in slavery are most severely persecuted, yet they persevere in spite of terrors and threats. But the Lord has given grace to many of my handmaids, for they zealously imitate him as far as they are able.

Therefore, though I could have wished to leave them, and had been ready and very desirous to go to Britannia, as if to my country and parents, and not that alone, but to go even to Gallia, to visit my brethren, and to see the face of my Lord's saints; and God knows that I desired it greatly. But I am bound in the spirit, and he who witnesseth will account me guilty if I do it, and I fear to lose the labor which I have commenced—and not I, but the Lord Christ, who commanded me to come and be with them for the rest of my life; if the Lord grants it, and keeps me from every evil way, that I should not sin before him. But I hope that which I am bound to do, but I trust not myself as long as I am in this body of death, for he is strong who daily tries to turn me from the faith, and from the sincere religious chastity to Christ my Lord, to which I have dedicated myself to the end of my life, but the flesh, which is in enmity, always draws me to death—that is, to unlawful desires, that must be unlawfully gratified—and I know in part that I have not led a perfect life like other believers. But I confess to my Lord, and do not blush before him, because I tell the truth, that from the time I knew him in my youth the love of God and his fear increased within me, and until now, by the favor of the Lord, I have kept the faith.

Let him who pleases insult and laugh at me; I will not be silent, neither do I conceal the signs and wonders that the Lord hath shown to me many years before they took place, as he who knew all things even before the world began. Therefore I ought to give thanks to God without ceasing, who often pardoned my uncalled-for folly and negligence, who did not let his anger turn fiercely against me, who allowed me to work with him, though I did not promptly follow what was shown me and what the Spirit suggested; and the Lord had compassion on me among thousands and thousands, because he saw my good-will; but then I knew not what to do, because many were hindering my mission, and were talking behind my back, and saying: "Why does he run into danger among enemies who know not God?" This was not said with malice, but because they did not approve of it, but, as I now testify, because of my rusticity, you understand; and I did not at once recognize the grace which was then in me, but now *I know I should have known before.*

Therefore, I have simply related to my brethren and fellow-servants who have believed in me why I have preached and still preach to strengthen and confirm your faith. Would that you also might aim at higher things and succeed better. This shall be my glory, because a wise son is the glory of his father. You know and God knows how I have lived among you from my youth up, both faithful in truth and sincere in heart; also, I have given the faith to the people among whom I dwell, and I will continue to do so. God knows I have not overreached any of them, nor do I think of it, because of God and his Church, lest I should excite persecution for them and all of us, and lest the name of the Lord should be blasphemed through me; for it is written, "Woe to the man through whom the name of the Lord is blasphemed." For though I am unskilled in names, I have endeavored to be careful even with my Christian brethren, and the virgins of Christ, and devout women, who freely gave me gifts, and cast of their ornaments upon the altar; but I returned them, though they were offended with me because I did so. But I, for the hope of immortality, guarded myself cautiously in all things, so that they could not find me unfaithful, even in the smallest matter, so that unbelievers could not defame or detract from my ministry in the least.

But when it happened that I baptized so many thousand men, did I expect even half a "screpall" from them? Tell me, and I will return it to you. Or when the Lord ordained clergy through my humility and ministry, did I confer the grace gratuitously? If I asked of any of them even the value of my shoe, tell me, and I will repay you more. I rather spent for you as far as I was able; and among you and everywhere for you I endured many perils in distant places, where none had been further or had ever come to baptize, or ordain the clergy, or confirm the people. By the grace of the Lord I labored freely and diligently in all things for your salvation. At this time also I used to give rewards to kings, whose sons I hired, who travelled with me, and who understood nothing but [to protect] me and my companions. And on one day they wished to kill me; but the time had not come yet; but they put me in irons and carried off all we possessed. But on the fourteenth day the Lord released me from their power, and what was ours was restored to us through God and through the friends we had before secured.

You know how much I expended on the judges in the districts which I visited most frequently. For I think I paid them not less than the hire of fifteen men, that you might have the benefit of my presence, and that I might always enjoy you in the Lord. I do not regret it, nor is it sufficient for me. I still spend, and will still spend, for your souls.] Behold, I call God to witness on my soul that I do not lie, neither that you may have occasion, nor that I hope for honor from any of you; sufficient for me is the honor of truth. But I see that now in the present world I am greatly exalted by the Lord; and I was not worthy nor fit to be thus exalted, for I know that poverty and calamity are more suitable for me than riches and luxury. But even Christ the Lord was poor for us.

Truly, I, a poor and miserable creature, even if I wished for wealth, have it not; neither do I judge myself, because I daily expect either death, or treachery, or slavery, or an occasion of some kind or another. [But I fear none of these things, relying on the heavenly promise; for I have cast myself into the hands of the omnipotent God, who rules everywhere; as the prophet says: "Cast thy care upon the Lord, and He shall sustain thee."

Behold, now I commend my soul to my most faithful God, whose mission I perform, notwithstanding my unworthiness; but because He does not accept persons, and has chosen me for this office, to be one of the least of His ministers. "What shall I render to Him for all the things that He hath rendered to me?" But what shall I say or promise to my Lord? For I see nothing unless He gives Himself to me; but He searches the heart and reins, because I ardently desire and am ready that He should give me to drink His cup, as He has permitted others to do who have loved Him. Wherefore may my Lord never permit me to lose His people whom He has gained in the ends of the earth. I pray God, therefore, that He may give me perseverance, and that He may vouchsafe to permit me to give Him faithful testimony for my God until my death. And if I have done anything good for my God, whom I love, I beseech Him to grant to me that with those proselytes and captives I may pour out my blood for His name, even if my body should be denied burial, and be miserably torn limb from limb by dogs or fierce beasts, or that the birds of heaven should devour it. I believe most certainly that if this should happen to me, I have gained both soul and body; for it is certain that we shall rise one day in the brightness of the sun—that is, the glory of Christ Jesus our Redeemer—as sons of God but as joint heirs with Christ, and to become conformable to His image.

For that sun which we see rises daily for us; but it will not rule or continue in its splendor forever, and all who adore it shall suffer very miserably. But we who believe in and adore the true sun, Christ, who will never perish, neither he who shall do His will, but even as Christ shall abide forever, who reigns with God the Father Almighty, and with the Holy Spirit, before the ages, and now, and for ever and ever. Amen.

Behold, again and again, I shall briefly declare the words of my confession. I testify in truth and in joy of heart, before God and His holy angels, that I never had any occasion, except the Gospel and its promises, for returning to that people from whom I had before with difficulty escaped.]

But I beseech those who believe in and fear God, whoever may condescend to look into or receive this writing, which Patrick, the ignorant sinner, has written in Ireland, that no one may ever say, if I have ever done or demonstrated anything, however little, that it was my ignorance. But do you judge, and let it be believed firmly, that it was the gift of God. And this is my confession before I die.

Thus far is what Patrick wrote with his own hand; he was translated to heaven on the seventeenth of March.

ST. PATRICK'S EPISTLE TO COROTICUS.

ST. PATRICK'S EPISTLE TO THE CHRISTIAN SUBJECTS OF THE TYRANT COROTICUS.

I, Patrick, a sinner and unlearned, have been appointed a bishop in Ireland, and I accept from God what I am. I dwell amongst barbarians as a proselyte and a fugitive for the love of God. He will testify that it is so. It is not my wish to pour forth so many harsh and severe things; but I am forced by zeal for God and the truth of Christ, who raised me up for my neighbors and sons, for whom I have forsaken my country and parents, and would give up even life itself, if I were worthy. I have vowed to my God to teach these people, though I should be despised by them, to whom I have written with my own hand to be given to the soldiers to be sent to Coroticus—I do not say to my fellow-citizens, nor to the fellow-citizens of pious Romans, but to the fellow-citizens of the devil, through their evil deeds and hostile practices. They live in death, companions of the apostate Scots and Picts, blood-thirsty men, ever ready to redden themselves with the blood of innocent Christians, numbers of whom I have begotten to God and confirmed in Christ.

On the day following that in which they were clothed in white and received the chrism of neophytes, they were cruelly cut up and slain with the sword by the above mentioned; and I sent a letter by a holy priest, whom I have taught from his infancy, with some clerics, begging that they would restore some of the plunder or the baptized captives; but they laughed at them. Therefore, I know not whether I should grieve most for those who were slain, or for those whom the devil insnared into the eternal pains of hell, where they will be chained like him. For whoever commits sin is the slave of sin, and is called the son of the devil.

Wherefore let every man know who fears God that they are estranged from me, and from Christ my God, whose ambassador I am—these patricides, fratricides, and ravening wolves, who devour the people of the Lord as if they were bread; as it is said: "The wicked have dissipated thy law," wherein in these latter times Ireland has been well and prosperously planted and instructed. Thanks be to God, I usurp nothing; I share with these whom He hath called and predestinated to preach the Gospel in much persecution, even to the ends of the earth.

But the enemy hath acted invidiously towards me through the tyrant Coroticus, who fears neither God nor His priests whom He hath chosen, and committed to them the high, divine power: "Whomsoever they shall bind on earth shall be bound in heaven."

I beseech you, therefore, who are the holy ones of God and humble of heart, that you will not be flattered by them, and that you will neither eat nor drink with them, nor receive their alms, until they do penance with many tears, and liberate the servants of God and the baptized hand-maids of Christ, for whom he was crucified and died. "He that offereth sacrifice of the goods of the poor, is as one that sacrificeth the son in the presence of the father." "Riches, he saith, which the unjust accumulate shall be vomited forth from his belly, the angel of death shall drag him away, he shall be punished with the fury of dragons, the tongue of the adder shall slay him, inextinguishable fire shall consume him." Hence, "Woe to those who fill themselves with things which are not their own." And "what doth it profit a man if he gain the whole world and suffer the loss of his soul?" It were too long to discuss one by one, or to select from the law, testimonies against such cupidity. Avarice is a mortal sin. "Thou shall not covet thy neighbor's goods." "Thou shall not kill." The homicide cannot dwell with Christ. "He who hateth his brother is a murderer," and "and he who loveth not his brother abideth in death." How much more guilty is he who hath defiled his hands with the blood of the sons of God, whom He hath recently acquired in the ends of the earth by our humble exhortations!

Did I come to Ireland according to God or according to the flesh? Who compelled me? I was led by the Spirit, that I should see my relatives no more. Have I not a pious mercy towards that nation which formerly took me captive? According to the flesh, I am of noble birth, my father being a Decurio. I do not regret or blush for having bartered my nobility for the good of others. I am a servant in Christ unto a foreign people for the ineffable glory of eternal life, which is in Christ Jesus my Lord; though my own people do not acknowledge me: "A prophet is without honor in his own country." Are we not from one stock, and have we not one God for our Father? As He has said: "He that is not with me is against me, and he that gathereth not with me scattereth." Is it not agreed that one pulleth down and another buildeth? I seek not my own.

Not to me be praise, but to God, who hath put into my heart this desire that I should be one of the hunters and fishers whom, of old, God hath announced should appear in the last days. I am reviled—what shall I do, O Lord? I am greatly despised. Lo! thy sheep are torn around me, and plundered by the above-mentioned robbers, aided by the soldiers of Coroticus: the betrayers of Christians into the hands of the Picts and Scots are far from the charity of God. Ravening wolves have scattered the flock of the Lord, which, with the greatest diligence, was increasing in Ireland; the sons of the Irish and the daughters of kings who are monks and virgins of Christ are too many to enumerate. Therefore, the oppression of the great is not pleasing to thee now, and never shall be.

Who of the saints would not dread to share in the feasts or amusements of such persons? They fill their houses with the spoils of the Christian dead, they live by rapine, they know not the poison, the deadly food, which they present to their friends and children; as Eve did not understand that she offered death to her husband, so are all those who work evil: they labor to work out death and eternal punishment.

It is the custom of the Christians of Rome and Gaul to send holy men to the Franks and other nations, with many thousand solidi, to redeem baptized captives. You who slay them, and sell them to foreign nations ignorant of God, deliver the members of Christ, as it were, into a den of wolves. What hope have you in God? Whoever agrees with you, or commands you, God will judge him. I know not what I can say, or what I can speak more of the departed sons of God slain cruelly by the sword. It is written: "Weep with them that weep." And again: "If any member suffers anything, all the members suffer with it." Therefore, the Church laments and bewails her sons and daughters, not slain by the sword, but sent away to distant countries, where sin is more shameless and abounds. There free-born Christian men are sold and enslaved amongst the wicked, abandoned, and apostate Picts.

Therefore, I cry out with grief and sorrow. O beautiful and well-beloved brethren and children! whom I have brought forth in Christ in such multitudes, what shall I do for you? I am not worthy before God or man to come to your assistance. The wicked have prevailed over us. We have become outcasts. It would seem that they do not think we have one baptism and one Father, God. They think it an indignity that we have been born in Ireland; as He said: "Have ye not one God? Why do ye each forsake his neighbor?" Therefore, I grieve for you—I grieve, O my beloved ones! But, on the other hand, I congratulate myself I have not labored for nothing—my journey has not been in vain. This horrible and amazing crime has been permitted to take place. Thanks be to God, ye who have believed and have been baptized have gone from earth to paradise. Certainly, ye have begun to migrate where there is no night or death or sorrow; but ye shall exult like young bulls loosed from their bonds and tread down the wicked under your feet as dust.

Truly, you shall reign with the apostles and prophets and martyrs, and obtain the eternal kingdom, as He hath testified, saying: "They shall come from the east and the west, and shall sit down with Abraham and Isaac and Jacob in the kingdom of heaven." Without are dogs, and sorcerers, and murderers, and liars, and perjurers, and they shall have their part in the everlasting lake of fire. Nor does the apostle say without reason: "If the just are scarcely saved, where shall the sinner, the impious, and the transgressor of the law appear?" Where will Coroticus and his wicked rebels against Christ find themselves when they shall see rewards distributed amongst the baptized women? What will he think of his miserable kingdom, which shall pass away in a moment, like clouds or smoke, which are dispersed by the wind? So shall deceitful sinners perish before the face of the Lord, and the just shall feast with great confidence with Christ, and judge the nations, and rule over unjust kings, for ever and ever. Amen.

I testify before God and His angels that it shall be so, as He hath intimated to my ignorance. These are not my words that I have set forth in Latin, but those of God and the prophets and apostles, who never lied: "He that believeth shall be saved, but he that believeth not shall be condemned."

God hath said it. I entreat whosoever is a servant of God that he be a willing bearer of this letter, that he be not drawn aside by any one, but that he shall see it read before all the people in the presence of Coroticus himself, that, if God inspire them, they may sometime return to God, and repent, though late; that they may liberate the baptized captives, and repent for their homicides of the Lord's brethren; so that they may deserve of God to live and to be whole here and hereafter. The peace of the Father, and of the Son, and of the Holy Ghost. Amen.

THE HYMN, OR 'ST. PATRICK'S BREASTPLATE.'

1.

I BIND myself[2] to-day,

To a strong power, an invocation[3] of the Trinity,
I believe in a Threeness with confession of a Oneness in[4] the Creator of Judgment.[5]

2.

I bind myself to-day,
To the power[6] of the birth of Christ, with His baptism,
To the power of the crucifixion, with His burial,
To the power or His resurrection, with His ascension.
To the power of His coming to the judgment of doom.

3.

I bind myself to-day,
To the power of the ranks of cherubim,[7]Col. i. 16.
In the obedience of angels,Heb. i. 14.
In the service of archangels,[8]Rev. xxii. 9.
In the hope of resurrection unto reward,Acts xxiii. 6.
In the prayers of patriarchs,[9]Gen. xxviii. 20.
In the predictions of prophets,1 Pet. i. 12.
In the preachings of apostles.Matt. xxviii. 19, 20.
In the faiths of confessors,[10]Acts vii. 55–60.
In the purity of holy virgins.Rev. xiv. 4.
In the acts of righteous men.Matt. V. 16.

4.

I bind myself to-day,
To the power of heaven, Psa. cxlviii. 1.
The light of sun,
The brightness of moon,[11]Psa. cxlviii. 3.
The splendour of fire,
The speed of lightning,[12] Psa. cxlviii. 7, 8.

The swiftness of wind, Psa. civ. 4.
The depth of the sea,
The stability of earth, Psa. civ. 5.
The firmness of rocks.[13]

5.

I bind myself to-day,
To the power of God to guide me, Deut. xxxiii. 27.
The might of God to uphold me,
The wisdom of God to teach me, Col. iii. 16.
The eye of God to watch over me,
The ear of God to hear me,
The word of God to speak for me,[14]1 Pet. iv. 11.
The hand of God to protect me,
The way of God to lie before me,[15]
The shield of God to shelter me,Psa. xviii. 1, 2.
The host of God to defend me,2 Kings vi. 17.
Against the snares of demons,
Against the temptations of vices,
Against [the lusts[16]] of nature, Eph. vi. 10-17.
Against every man who meditates injury to me,
Whether far or near,
Alone and in a multitude.[17]

6.

I summon to-day[18] around me all these powers,
Against every hostile merciless power directed against my body and my
soul.Jude 20.
Against the incantations of false prophets,Acts xiii. 8–12.
Against the black laws of heathenism,
Against the false laws of heretics,[19]
Against the deceit of idolatry,1 John v. 21.
Against the spells of women, and smiths, and Druids,
Against all knowledge which hath defiled man's body and soul.[20]Jude
10.

7.

Christ protect me to-day,
Against poison, against burning, Mark xvi. 18.
Against drowning, against wound, Acts xxviii. 22–25.

That I may receive a multitude of rewards. Heb. x. 35.

8.

Christ with me, Christ before me,
Christ behind me, Christ within me,
Christ beneath me, Christ above me,
Christ at my right, Christ at my left,
Christ in breadth, Christ in length, Christ in height.[21] Eph. iii. 18, 19.

9.

Christ in the heart of every man who thinks of me,
Christ in the mouth of every man who speaks to me,
Christ in the eye of every man that sees me,
Christ in the ear of every man that hears me.

10.

I bind myself to-day.
To a strong power, an invocation of the Trinity,
I believe in a Threeness with confession of a Oneness in the Creator of Judgment.[22]

11.

Salvation is the Lord's,Psa. iii. 8.
Salvation is the Lord's,
Salvation is Christ's,Rev. vii. 10.
Let Thy salvation, O Lord, be ever with us.[23]Isa. xxv. 9.

1.

2.   The figures refer to the notes at the end of the book.

3.   The following is the Irish preface to the Hymn found in the Liber Hymnorum, Trinity College, Dublin, folio 196. The translation is given, with the original Irish, on p. 381 of the Rolls *Triparite Life of St. Patrick*. We quote it as a curiosity, and nothing more, not, of course, endorsing the truth of the legend referred to.

4.   'Patrick made this hymn. In the time of Loegaire, son of Niall, it was made. Now, the cause of making it was to protect himself with his monks against the deadly enemies who were in ambush against the clerics. And this is a corslet of faith for the protection of body and soul against devils and human beings and vices. Whosoever shall sing it every day, with pious meditation on God, devils will not stay before him. It will be a safeguard to him against all poison and envy. It will be a defence to him against sudden death. It will be a corslet to his soul after dying. Patrick chanted this when the ambushes were set against him by Loegaire, that he might not go to Tara to sow the faith, so that there they seemed before the liers-in-wait to be wild deer, with a fawn behind them, to wit, Benén. And *Fâed Fiada* ("Deer's Cry") is its name.'

5. According to the story set forth in the Rolls *Tripartite Life* (p. 48), Patrick, with eight young clerics and Benén, his faithful servant or gillie, sometimes called his 'foster-son' (*Tripartite*, p. 144), passed safely through all the men who were lying in wait for them on the occasion of his visit to Tara. The persons lying in ambush saw only eight deer running away, and a fawn after them, which was Benén.

6. 'The first word of this hymn *Atomriug* was mistaken by Dr. Petrie and Dr. O'Donovan for an obsolete form of the dative of *Temur*, Temoria or Tara, and was by them translated "*At Tara*." We cannot now regret this error, as to it we owe the publication of this curious poem in the *Essay on Tara*. But it is certainly a mistake, and was acknowledged as such by Dr. O'Donovan before his death. The word is a verb; *ad-domriug*, i.e., *ad-riug, adjungo*, with the infixed pronoun *dom*, "to me" (see Zeuss, Gram. Celt. p. 336); the verb *riug*, which occurs in the forms *ad-riug, con-riug*, signifies "to join."' (Dr. Todd's *St. Patrick*, p. 426.) The true analysis of the word was first pointed out by Dr. Whitley Stokes in the *Saturday Review*, September 5, 1857, p. 225.

7. 'Drs. O'Donovan and Petrie translate the original word *togairm, invoco*, but it is a substantive, not a verb.' (*Todd*, p. 46.)

8. Dr. Todd thought *cretim* in this line was a noun, but it is obviously the common verb, *i.e.*, the Latin *credo*. The word for 'Threeness' is different from that for 'Trinity,' hence we have followed Dr. Whitley Stokes' new version. The sense is the same as that given in our former edition, 'the faith of the Trinity in Unity,' only fuller in expression. *Fóisin* in this line was rendered by Petrie '*under the*.' But the correct reading is *fóisitin*, the instrumental sing. 'with the confession.' (See the Rolls *Tripartite Life*, pp. 48, 650.)

9. The original is *dail*, genitive sing. of *dal*, 'judgment,' 'doom,' as in *dal bâis*, 'doom of death,' *Leber na hUidre*, p. 118 b., not *dúile*, 'elements,' as generally given. (See the Rolls *Tripartite*, pp. 566, 645.) Patrick seems to have had in mind the passage in Isaiah xlv. 7, where the words 'I make peace and create evil' [Vulg. *et creans malu*.] are used of God as 'the Creator of judgment.' Comp. Amos iii. 6.

10. The expression in the Hymn 'the Creator of Judgment' or 'Creator of Doom,' appears to afford an undesigned evidence of the Patrician authorship of the poem. 'God of Judgment' (*dar moDla mbratha—Lebar Brecc* in the *Rolls Tripartite*, p. 460) was a favourite expression of Patrick (compare Isaiah xxx. 18, Malachi ii. 17, *Deus judicii*). Compare his saying: '*I cannot judge, but God will judge*.' (Rolls *Tripartite*, p. 288.) Another expression, '*My God's doom!* or '*judgment*' (*mo debrod, mo debroth*), was constantly in his mouth. (See the Rolls *Tripartite*, pp. 132, 138, 142, 168, 174, &c.) It is explained in the extraft from Cormac's Glossary, p. 571. The thoughts of the saint, on his way to Tara, must necessarily have dwelt much on the judgment and doom of idolaters in 'the day of vengeance of our God' (Isa. lxi. 2). The Irish for the 'judgment of doom' in the last line of the second stanza of the Hymn is *brethemnas bratha*. Hence we have used a different English word in these places to express the difference in the original Irish.

11. Dr. Whitley Stokes has throughout 'virtue' in place of 'power.'

12. The original is *grad hiruphin*, which is thus rendered by Dr. Whitley Stokes. The former translation was 'the love of seraphim.'

13. This line is not in the Trinity College Liber Hymnorum. It is taken from the Bodleian copy.

14. Dr. Todd renders 'in the prayers of the noble fathers.' Hennessy and Dr. Whitley Stokes, 'patriarchs.'

15. The original has 'in the preachings' of apostles and 'in the faiths of confessors' in the plural, instead of 'preaching' and 'faith.'

16. So the Bodleian copy. The Trinity College MS. has *etrochta snechtai*, i.e., 'whiteness of snow.'

17. The line was formerly translated 'the force of tire, the flashing of lightning.

18. Dr. Whitley Stokes would render 'firmness' or 'steadiness of rock.'

19. So Dr. Whitley Stokes. The former translation was 'to give me speech.' Comp. 1 Peter iv. 11.

20. So Dr. Whitley Stokes. The former version was 'to prevent me.'

21. The translation of the word 'the lusts' is uncertain, and consequently there is a blank left here in Dr. Whitley Stokes' version.

22. So Dr. Whitley Stokes. The former translation was 'with few or with many,' which gives almost the same sense.

23. Dr. Whitley Stokes has 'I summon to-day all these virtues between me [and these evils].' Dr. Todd's translation is 'I have set around me.'

24. So Dr. Whitley Stokes, as the Irish is *heretecda*. There are slight verbal changes in his translation here which are of little importance.

25. Dr. Todd's translation is 'which blinds the soul of man,' the Trinity College MS. saying nothing of man's body (*corp*).

26.   So Dr. Whitley Stokes renders. The words are an imitation of Eph. iii, 18, 19, 'That ye being rooted and grounded in love, may be strong to apprehend with all the saints what is the breadth and length and height and depth, and to know the love of Christ which passeth knowledge.' The original in the Trinity College MS. is *Crist illius, Crist issius* [*ipsius* in the Bodleian MS.], *Crist inerus*. Dr. Whitley Stokes, in his *Goidelica* (2nd edit., London, 1872, p. 153), regards *lius* as a derivative of *leth* 'breadth'; *sius* as derived from *sith*, 'long'; and *erus* as a derivative of '*er*,' which is glossed by *uasal*. This Irish gloss is decisive, and shows the reference to be to Eph. iii. The words in the original have not yet been discovered elsewhere in old Irish. The former version was 'Christ in the fort, Christ in the chariot-seat, Christ in the poop,' and was explained to mean: Christ with me when I am at home; Christ with me when I am travelling by land, and in the ship when I am travelling by water. The Irish words were formerly explained: *lius* as dat. sing. of *les*, 'fort'; *sius* as dat. of *ses* cognate with *suidim*, 'I sit'; *erus* as dat. sing. of *eross*, 'poop.'

27.   See note 5.

28.   The original of this antiphon is in Latin, the rest of the hymn is in Irish. The last stanza is—

29.   Domini est salus, Domini est salus, Christi est salus,
Salus tua, Domine, sit semper nobiscum.

SAYINGS OF PATRICK.

T HE following *Dicta Patricii*, or Sayings of St. Patrick, are given in Latin in the Rolls edition of the *Tripartite Life*, p. 301, as contained at the end of the Notes by Muirchu Maccu-Machtheni in the Book of Armagh, fol. 9, a. i. They are, as Dr. Whitley Stokes observes, disconneded from the context in that MS., with the simple heading *Dicta Patricii*, and are in very rustic Latin. The character of their Latinity renders it highly probable that they may be genuine remains of the saint, while the manner in which the Greek Κύριε ἐλέισον (*Lord, have mercy on us*) is transliterated into Latin (in Sayings No. 4 and 5) is sufficient to show how slight an acquaintance Patrick had with the Greek language. The latter point confutes Nicholson's arguments (on pp. 84, 85, 168 of his work), in which he seeks to prove that 'St. Patrick read the Scriptures from the Greek language alone.'

We have for convenience sake numbered the Sayings, and append them here, with the addition of a few notes:—

1. 'I had the fear of God as the guide of my journey through the Gauls [*per Gallias*] and Italy, even in the islands which are in the Tyrrhenian Sea.'
The latter portion of this saying, from 'through the Gauls,' is incorporated into Tirechan's notes or collections of facts concerning Patrick found in the Book of Armagh. (Rolls edition, p. 302.) Dr. W. Stokes says that these notes are said to have been 'written from the dictation or copied from a book (*ex ore vel libra*) of his foster-father or tutor. Bishop Altán of Ardbraccan, who died A.D. 656.' (Rolls edition of *Tripartite Life*, p. xci.) If the 'saying' be genuine, Patrick must have visited Italy. But the evidence is weak, and will not bear much weight to be put upon it.

2. 'From the world ye have passed on to Paradise.'
The saying quoted occurs in the *Epistle to Coroticus*, §9, p. 78.

3. 'Thanks be to God!'
This saying, which is found in the *Coroticus*, p. 78, and in the *Confession*, pp. 54, 57, 64 (compare also pp. 60, 66, 68), is entitled, from the frequency of its occurrence, to be numbered separately. The saying is well illustrated by the following story, given by Muirchu in his Notes on St. Patrick's Life (which are of the seventh century). Dáire, the Irish chieftain, who afterwards gave the

site for a church at Armagh, sent to the saint as a present a caldron of brass which had been imported from across the sea. Patrick, on receiving the gift, said simply, *Grazacham* (*gratias agamus*, 'Let us give thanks,' *i.e.*, to God). Dáire went back to his home, muttering, 'The man is a fool who said nothing but *grazacham* for a brazen caldron of such a size!' He then ordered his servants to go and bring him back the caldron. They went forthwith to the saint, and said, 'We are going to take away the caldron.' Patrick said again, '*Grazachm*, take it away.' They accordingly took it back. When they returned, Dáire asked them, 'What did the Christian say when you took it away?' They answered that he said, '*Grazacham*.' Dáire exclaimed, '*Grazacham*, when it was given! *grazacham*, when it was taken away! his saying is so good with those *grazachams*, that his caldron shall be brought back to him again!' (Rolls *Tripartite*, p. 291.) The same story is repeated in the *Tripartite Life* (which was written in the eleventh century) at pp. 230, 231 of the Rolls edition. See also Miss Cusack's *Life of St. Patrick*, p. 351, Dr. Todd's *Life*, p. 471. On the story, compare the words in Job i. 21: 'The Lord gave, and the Lord hath taken away; blessed be the name of the Lord.'

4. The Church of the Scots, nay even of the Romans, (chant) as Christians, so, that ye may be Romans, (chant) as it ought to be chanted with you, at every hour of prayer that praiseworthy sentence. *Curie lession, Christe lession* ["Lord, have mercy upon us," "Christ have mercy upon us."].'
The Latin is: 'Aeclessia Scotorum, immo Romanorum, ut Christiani, ita ut Romani sitis, ut decantetur uobiscum oportet omni hora orationis uox illa laudabilis "Curie lessión, Christe lession."' It is evidently corrupt with its three "ut"s. Dr. Whitley Stokes has suggested to me that it should be read thus: 'Aeclessia Scottorum immo Romanorum, ut Christiani ita et Romani sitis, et decantetur vobiscum ut oportet omni hora orationis vox illa laudabilis,' &c. It should then be translated:—

'Church of the Scots, nay of the Romans, as ye are Christians so also be Romans; and let that praiseworthy sentence be chanted by you at every (canonical) hour, as it ought to be, "Lord, have mercy upon us, Christ, have mercy upon us."'

It must not be forgotten that in the *Epistle to Coroticus* Patrick speaks of himself as a Roman and a freeman (see *Coroticus*, p. 76). He also there alludes to 'the Roman and Gallic Christians' as superior to other Christians in civilisation. It is most natural, therefore, to interpret the meaning of this saying to be: Imitate the customs of those Christians whose higher civilisation is a matter of general acknowledgment, and follow their example by making use of the versicle in question.

5. 'Let every Church that follows me chant, "Curie lession, Christe lession." Thanks be to God!'

The words quoted by St. Patrick in these two 'sayings' are Κύριε ἐλέεισον, Χρίστε ἐλ εισον.

PROVERBS OF PATRICK.

THE following twelve sayings, styled *Proverbia St. Patricii*, are given by Villanueva (see Introduction, p. 12), as, according to Jocelin, having been translated into Latin from the Irish. All these 'sayings,' with others, are also given in Latin in the 'Extracts from the Irish Canons' in the Rolls *Tripartite*, p. 507 ff. Their authenticity is, however, somewhat questionable, although the Biblical quotations are curiously similar to those found in the genuine writings.

1. 'Patrick says: "It is better for us to admonish the negligent, that crimes may not abound, than to blame the things that have been done." Solomon says: "It is better to reprove than to be angry."'
The passage referred to is, however, not found in the Solomonic writings, but occurs in Ecclesiasticus (the Book of Jesus the Son of Sirach) xx. 1. The Latin, *melius est arguere quam irasci*, is different from the Vulg. and the Itala, *quam bonum est arguere quam irasci.*

2. 'Patrick says: "Judges of the Church ought not to have the fear of man, but the fear of God, because the fear of God is the beginning of wisdom" (Prov. i. 7).'

3. 'Judges of the Church ought not to have the wisdom of this world, "for the wisdom of this world is foolishness with God," but to have the "wisdom of God" (1 Cor. iii. 19; i. 21).'

4. 'Judges of the Church ought not to take gifts, because "gifts blind the eyes of the wise, and change the words of the just."'
The passage referred to is Ecclesiasticus xx. 31, but the quotation is not exact. The words quoted by Patrick are, *munera excæcant oculos sapientium et mutant verba justorum.* The Itala and Vulgate have: *Xenia et dona excæcant oculos judicum, et quasi mutus in ore avertit correptiones corum, i.e.,* 'Presents and gifts blind the eyes of judges, and make them dumb in the mouth, so that they cannot correct.' (*Douay Version.*) The rendering of the latter clause in the Douay Version is a paraphrase of the Latin and Greek.

5. 'Judges of the Church ought not to respect a person in judgment, "for there is no respect of persons with God" (Rom. ii. 11).'

6. 'Judges of the Church ought not to have worldly wisdom (*cautelam sæcularem*) but Divine examples (before them), for it does not become the servant of God to be crafty or cunning (*cautum aut astutum*).'
Villanueva explains *cautela sæcularis* as equivalent to the *sapientia carnis*, 'the wisdom of the flesh,' or 'carnal wisdom,' of Rom. viii. 7. Compare 1 Cor. iii. 19.

7. 'Judges of the Church ought not to be so swift in judgment until they know how too true it may be which is written, "Do not desire quickly to be a judge."'
The passage cited is Eccles. vii. 6. The quotation is slightly different from the Vulg. Patrick quotes the words, *noli judex esse cito*. The Jtala and Vulg. have, *noli quærere fieri iudex*, 'Seek not to be made a judge.' (*Douny Version.*)

8. 'Judges of the Church ought not to be voluble.'
The doctrine of St. Patrick here is akin to that in James i. 19, 20.

9. 'Judges of the Church ought not to tell a lie, for a lie is a great crime.'
Compare John viii. 44; Eph. iv. 25; Rev. xxii. 15.

10. 'Judges of the Church ought to "judge just judgment," "for with whatever judgment they shall judge, it shall be judged to them."'
The first passage quoted is from John vii. 24. The second passage is from Matt. vii. 2. Patrick quotes the latter: *in quocunque judicio judicaverint, judicabitur de illis*. The Vulgate is, *in quo enim judicio judicaveritis, judicabimini*, 'for with what judgment you judge, you shall be judged.' Similarly the Itala.

11. ' Patrick says: "Look into the examples of the elders, where you will find no guile."'
The Latin is: *exempla majorum perquire ubi nihil fallaciæ invenies*. By 'the elders' Villanueva considers Patrick means the saints, apostles, evangelists, and disciples of the Lord, and the fathers and doctors of the Church.

12. 'Patrick says: "Judges who do not judge rightly the judgments of the Church are not judges, but falsifiers (*falsatores*)."'

THE STORY OF PATRICK AND THE ROYAL DAUGHTERS.

THE following story, which is given in Tirechan's collection, found in the Book of Armagh, bears internal evidence of its antiquity and genuineness. 'The naïveté of the questions asked by the girls about God and His sons and daughters' is one of these striking evidences, for they are, as Whitley Stokes observes, 'questions which no mere legend-monger ever had the imagination to invent.' The narrative is quite superior to the surroundings in which it occurs in Tírechán (Rolls *Tripartite*, p. 314), or in the later *Tripartite Life* (pp. 99 ff.). We have translated it from the former, adding in the notes the more important readings found in the *Tripartite Life*.

But thence went the holy Patrick to the spring which is called Clebach,[1] on the sides of Crochan,[2] towards the rising of the sun, before the rising of the sun, and they sat beside the springs. And behold two daughters of Loegaire,[3] Ethne the fair, and Fedelm the ruddy, came to the spring in the morning, after the custom of women, to wash,[4] and they found a holy synod of bishops with Patrick by the spring.[5] And they did not know from whence they were, or of what shape, or of what people, or of what region. But they thought that they were men of the *side*, or of the terrestrial gods, or an apparition.[6] And the daughters said to them—

'Whence are ye, and whence have ye come?'

And Patrick said to them—

'It were better that you would confess our true God than to inquire about our race.'

The first daughter said, 'Who is God? And where is God? And of what is God? And where is His dwelling-place? Has your God sons and daughters, gold and silver? Is He ever-living? Is He beautiful? Have many fostered His Son? Are His daughters dear and beautiful to the men or the world? Is He in heaven or on earth? In the sea? in the rivers? in the mountains? in the valleys? Tell us how is He seen? How is He loved? How is He found? Is He in youth? or in age?'[7]

But holy Patrick, full of the Holy Spirit, answering, said—

'Our God is the God of all men, the God of heaven and earth, of the sea, and of the rivers; the God of the sun and of the moon, of all the stars; the God of the lofty mountains and of the lowly valleys; the God over heaven and in heaven and under heaven. He has His dwelling towards heaven and earth, and the sea, and all things which are in them. He inspires all things, He gives life to all things, He surpasses all things, He supports all things. He kindles the light of the sun, He strengthens the light of the moon at night for watches;[8] and He made springs in the arid land, and dry islands in the sea; and the stars He placed to minister to the greater lights. He has a Son co-eternal with Himself and like unto Himself. The Son is not younger than the Father, nor is the Father older than the Son. The Father, Son, and Holy Spirit are not separated. I truly desire to unite you to the Heavenly King, since ye are daughters of an earthly king. Believe (on Him).'

And the daughters said, as if with one mouth and heart—

'How can we believe on the Heavenly King? Teach us most diligently, so that we may see Him face to face. Point out to us, and we will do whatsoever thou shalt say to us.'

And Patrick said: 'Do you believe that the sin of your father and mother is taken away by baptism?

'They replied: 'We do believe it.'

[*Patrick*] 'Do you believe that there is repentance after sin?'

[*Daughters*] 'We do believe it.'

[*Patrick*] 'Do you believe that there is a life after death? Do you believe in the resurrection in the day of judgment?'

[*Daughters*] 'We do believe it.'

[*Patrick*] 'Do you believe in the unity of the Church?'

[*The Daughters*] 'We do believe it.'

And they were baptized, and [Patrick placed] a white garment[9] on their heads.

And they begged to see the face of Christ.

And the saint said to them: 'Unless you shall have tasted death, you cannot see the face of Christ, and unless you shall receive the sacrifice.'[10]

And they replied: 'Give to us the sacrifice, that we may see the Son our spouse.'

And they received the Eucharist of God, and they slept in death. And they placed them in a bed covered with one mantle, and their friends made a wailing and a great lamentation. . . . And the days of the wailing for the daughters of the king were ended, and they buried them by the spring *Clebach*, and they made a round ditch in the likeness of a *ferta* [*a grave*], because so the Scotic men and Gentiles used to do. But, with us it is called *relic*, that is, the *remains* and *feurt*.

The latter few lines of the story are slightly different in the *Tripartite Life*. It will be observed that the doctrine set forth with regard to the two sacraments is somewhat questionable. But it must be remembered that errors on those points were prevalent in the Church of the fifth century. The story in general is one of considerable beauty, and is worthy to be preserved as a genuine fragment of a striking missionary incident in the early part of that century.

1. Cliabach. (*Trip.*)
2. Cruachan. (*Trip.*)
3. 'Loegaire, son of Niall.' (*Trip.*)
4. 'to wash their hands.' (*Trip.*)
5. 'the maidens found beside the well the assembly of clerics in white garments, with their books before them.' (*Trip.*)
6. 'And they wondered at the shape of the clerics, and thought that they were men of the elves or apparitions.' (*Trip.*) Dr. Whitley Stokes' note on Tírechán is, '*Firu síde*, "males of the *síde*" or terrestrial gods, corresponding, perhaps, with the θεοὶ χθόνιοι or Inferi.'
7. The questions are somewhat transposed in the *Tripartite Life*, but are substantially identical.
8. This is a conjectural translation. The Latin is [*lunæ*] *lumen noctis ad* [MS. *et*] *notitias valat.*
9. The white garment of baptism worn for eight days by the newly-baptized in the ancient church. See *Coroticus*, p. 68. Some Roman Catholic writers have endeavoured to explain this that the virgins took the veil, but that is not the meaning. See Dr. Todd's *St. Patrick*, p. 456.
10. Instead of 'the sacrifice,' the *Tripartite Life* has, 'unless ye receive Christ's body and His blood.'

www.ingramcontent.com/pod-product-compliance
Lightning Source LLC
Chambersburg PA
CBHW070957120626
46546CB00004B/1655